Anonymous

The Bristol Tune-Book

A Manual of Tunes and Chants

Anonymous

The Bristol Tune-Book
A Manual of Tunes and Chants

ISBN/EAN: 9783337395636

Printed in Europe, USA, Canada, Australia, Japan

Cover: Foto ©Thomas Meinert / pixelio.de

More available books at **www.hansebooks.com**

THE

𝕭𝖗𝖎𝖘𝖙𝖔𝖑 𝕮𝖚𝖓𝖊-𝕭𝖔𝖔𝖐.

A MANUAL

OF

TUNES AND CHANTS.

"LET ALL THE PEOPLE PRAISE THEE."
Psalm lxvii. 8.

LONDON:
NOVELLO, EWER AND CO., 1, BERNERS STREET, AND 35, POULTRY.

BRISTOL: W. AND F. MORGAN.

PREFACE.

THE Compilers of the Bristol Tune Book originally contemplated the convenience of congregations with which they are connected, by supplying, in a single volume, a complete selection of the best Tunes and Chants; hence its local appellation. Their object was, to produce a work sufficiently comprehensive, varied as to style, correct in harmony, and systematically arranged for practical use; which, while containing many compositions of such beauty as to repay the attention of practised choirs, should not be beyond the attainment of most congregations.

Finding, in the course of enquiry, that the want of such a book was by no means peculiar to their own locality, and encouraged by the generous courtesy with which composers and proprietors of existing works have met their application for the use of valuable copyrights, they venture to dedicate the result of their efforts to the service of the Church generally.

They have much gratification in thus publicly acknowledging the very large amount of assistance they have received in the undertaking. Especially are they indebted to the Rev. W. H. Havergal, Canon of Worcester, the Rev. P. Maurice, D.D., the Rev. P. Latrobe, E. B. Fripp, Esq., H. Bemrose, Esq., and the Society for Promoting Christian Knowledge, for unrestricted use of their respective compilations; to the Rev. J. B. Dykes, Mus. Doc., Precentor of Durham Cathedral, A. H. Brown, Esq., Brentwood, J. Summers, Esq., Weston-super-Mare, and A. R. Reinagle, Esq., Oxford, for contributions of original Tunes and much valuable assistance; to the Lord Bishop of Argyll and the Isles, for permission to print tune No. 159; to the Lord Bishop of Ely for No. 93; to the Rev. Sir H. W. Baker, Bart., and the Compilers of "Hymns Ancient and Modern," the Rev. R. R. Chope, Rev. W. J. Blew, Rev. H. Allon, Rev. J. Curwen, Mr. E. Stock, and Messrs. T. Nelson and Sons, for permission to use several tunes from their excellent works; to the Cheadle Association for the Promotion of Church Music, for Mr. W. H. Monk's tune to the Easter-Hymn; to Dr. Steggall, M. Costa, Esq., and their Publishers, Messrs. Addison and Lucas, for tunes Nos. 92 and 104, from Dr. Steggall's Psalmody, for M. Costa's arrangement of the Chorale No. 144 from the *Eli*, and for liberty to adapt tune No. 105 from the same Oratorio; to the Proprietors of "Congregational Church Music" for No. 152, and for arrangements of Nos. 8, 31, 44, 71, 193, and 256; and to those of the "Psalmist" for Nos. 85 and 89; to Messrs. Novello and Co., for kindly allowing the use of Nos. 54, 76, 87, 102, 145, 191, 202, 209, 214, 238, 243, and 255 (No. 2); to the Hon. and Rev. F. R. Grey, Rev. W. Jacobs, J. Goss, Esq., A. King, Esq., Dr. Henry Leslie, W. Woodward, Esq., G. A. Löhr, Esq., W. Mason, Esq., J. Daniell, Esq., J. Foster, Esq., and others, for tunes which bear their names; to W. R. Braine, Esq., Dr. Gauntlett, Messrs. Masters and Co., Messrs. Burns and Lambert, Messrs. Richardson and Sons, and others, for tunes for which consideration has been paid; to Mr. R. M. Mills, for Dr. Crotch's Chants; to Messrs. R. Cocks and Co., for Chant No. 331; to Mr. Masters, for the words of "Dies Iræ;" and, finally, for the kind permission, so courteously granted, to print the Chants bearing the name of A. H. D. Troyte.   Very many excellent friends have also sent original tunes which do not appear in the work; will they accept the assurance that their kindness is none the less appreciated?

This Manual being designed as a companion to the Hymnals already in use, a few Hymns only are printed complete, for which the accompanying tunes are either particularly suitable, or were specially composed; single verses are inserted where needful to indicate the metre, accent, or character of the music.

The Compilers have spared neither time, pains, nor expense in furtherance of their object, and will feel amply compensated if the result prove acceptable to the Church, and of use in the Service of Praise.

Bristol, Easter, 1863.

INDEX I.—METRICAL.

INDEX I.—METRICAL.

INDEX II.—ALPHABETICAL.

INDEX III.—CHANTS.

SINGLE.

Composer.	Key.	No.	Composer.	Key.	No.
Aldrich, H., D.D.	B♭	263	Hayes, Dr. Philip	F	273
Ayrton, Dr.	E♭	264	Hayes, Dr. W.	E	274
Battishill, J.	A	265	Humphrey, P. (Grand Chant)	C	275
Bellamy, R.	F	266	Kent, James	G	276
Blow, Dr. J.	E minor	267	Purcell, Henry	G	277
Cooke, Dr. B.	F	268		G minor	278
Croft, Dr. W.	A minor	269	Tallis, T.	C	279
Farrant, Richard	A „	270	„	F	280
	F „	271	Travers, John	E	281
Felton, Rev W.	F	272	Turner, Dr. W.	A	282

DOUBLE.

Composer.	Key.	No.	Composer.	Key.	No.
Alcock, Dr.	E♭	283	Jackson, William	B♭	309
Barrow, Isaac	G	284	Jacobs, Rev. W.	B♭	310
Battishill, J.	D	285	Jones, J.	D	311
„	A minor	286	Kemp, Dr.	E	312
Bennett, A.	F	287	Langdon, R., M.B.	E	313
Blount,	G	288		F	314
Boyce, Dr. W.	D	289	Lawes, Henry	C	315
Calah, J.	A	290	Leslie, Dr. Henry	D	316
Caley, Rev. R. L.	F	291		C minor	317
	B♭	292	Lingard, —	F	318
Chard, Dr. W.	A	293	Morley, T.	D minor	319
Charlot, T.	C	294	Mornington, Earl of	E	320
Cleveland, —	D	295		E♭	321
Cooke, Robert	G	296	Norris, T., M.B.	A	322
Cooke, Dr.	E minor	297	Pearson, H.	E	323
Crotch, Dr.	C	298	Randall, Dr.	D	324
„	G	299		E	325
„	E	300	Robinson, J.	E♭	326
Davy, J.	E♭	301	Rogers, Sir J. L.	G	327
Dupuis, Dr. T. S.	A	302	Russell, W., M.B.	E	328
Gibbons, O.	E♭	303	Smith, J. S.	A	329
Goodenough Rev. R. P.	B♭	304	Spohr, L.	F	330
Goss, J.	C minor	305	Warren, —	G	331
Handel, G. F.	G	306	Woodward, Dr.	C	332
Heathcote, Rev. G.	A	307			
Henley, Rev. P.	E	308	Gregorian Tones		333 to 342

1

Augustine. s.m.

J. S. Bach.

2

Bethlehem. s.m.

S. Wesley.

(1)

3　　　　　　　　**Clifton.**　s.m. (Prize tune.)

J. BRABHAM.

Organist of St. Thomas, Charterhouse, London.

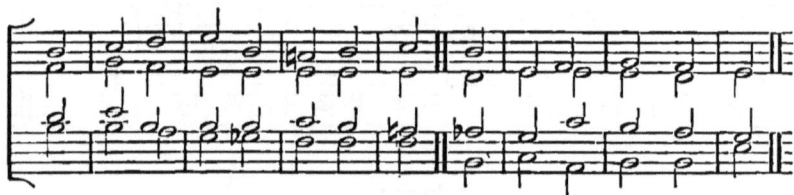

4　　　　　　　　**Eastnor.**　s.m.

A. KING, Ledbury.

(2)

5 *A & M 34* **Franconia.** s.m.

German Melody.

6 **Holy Rood.** s.m.

ARTHUR HENRY BROWN,
Organist of Brentwood, Essex.

7   **Huddersfield.**   s.m.

8   **Olmutz.**   s.m.

Dr. L. Mason.

(4)

9   **Serenity.**   s.m.

C. Bryan.

10   **Shawmut.**   s.m.

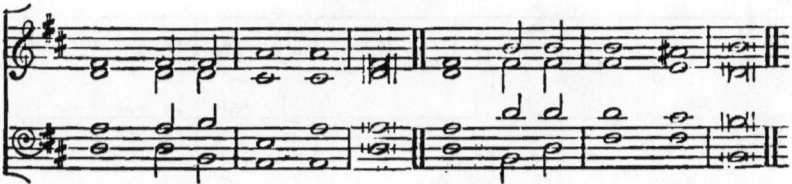

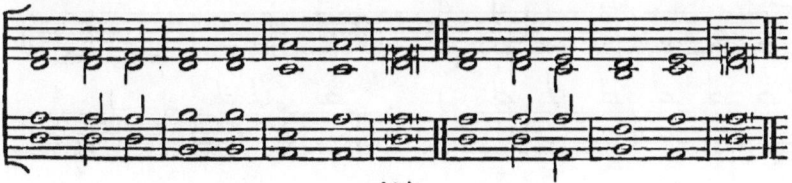

(5)

11   Silchester. s.m.

REV. DR. MALAN.

12   281 arm   Swabia. s.m.

German Melody.

(6)

13 *81 a 4m*   St. Bride. s.m.

DR. HOWARD.

14   St. John. s.m.

A. KING.

B

15   **St. Mary Redcliffe.**   s.m.

C. Bryan.

16   55 a 7m   **St. Michael.**   s.m.

Day's Psalter, 1588.

(8)

17

St. Raphael. s.m.

18

Thetford. s.m. (Prize tune.)

F. C. ATKINSON,
Organist of St. John's, Bradford, Yorkshire

(9)

19   **Tuam.**   s.m

W. Mason.
Organist of Tuam Cathedral.

20   **Tytherton.**   s.m.

Rev. L. R. West.

21   **Abbey.**   c.m.

Scotch Psalter, 1615.

22   *334 a×m*   **Abridge.**   c.m.

ISAAC SMITH.

23 **Arnold's.** c.m., or 11.8.11.8.

Dr. Arnold.

24 *153 a & m* **Bedford.** c.m.

W. Wheall.

25 *S. alb. 109* **Belmont.** C.M.

S. WEBBE.

26 **Bristol.** C.M.

DR. HODGES.

(13)

27 30 a ꜰm **Chichester.** C.M.

Ravenscroft's Psalter, 1621

28 **Claremont.** C.M.

J: Foster, Bristol.

(14)

29   **Dublin.** c.m.

30 *27 a 4 m*   **Dundee.** c.m.

31

Eban. C.M.

Dr. L. Mason.

32

Farrant. C.M.

R. Farrant.

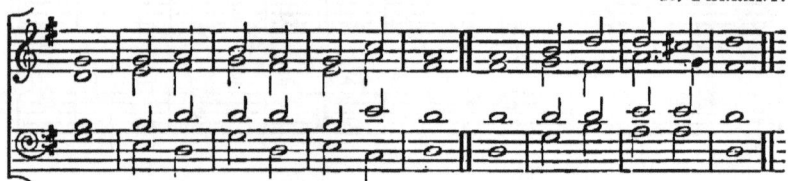

33
Gloucester. c.m.

Ravenscroft's Psalter, 1621.

34 _a & m 192._ **London.** c.m.

Dr. Croft.

35 **Manchester.** C. M.

Dr. Wainwright.

36 **Martyrdom.** C.M.

Hugh Wilson.

(18)

37 α 4m 301(ii) **Miles' Lane.** C.M.P.

All hail the pow'r of Je-su's name, Let au-gels prostrate fall; Bring forth the

Roy-al Di - a - dem, And crown Him, crown Him, crown Him, crown Him Lord of all.

38 **Mylon.** C M.

Palestine. c.m.

J. Sumners

Rome. c.m.

By permission of Burns and Lambert.

41 **Salisbury.** c.m.

Ravenscroft's Psalter, 1621.

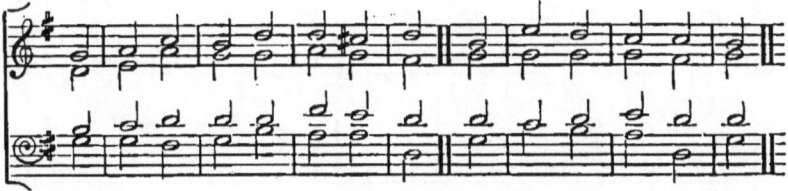

42 **Solomon.** c.m.

From HANDEL.

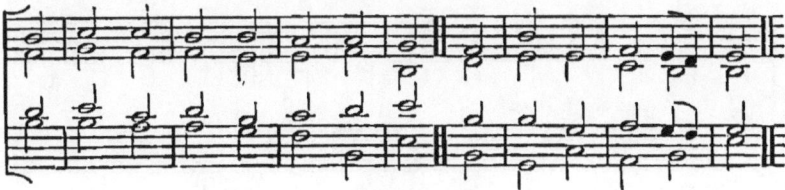

(21)

43

Southampton. C.M.

DR. CROFT

44

Sprague. C.M.

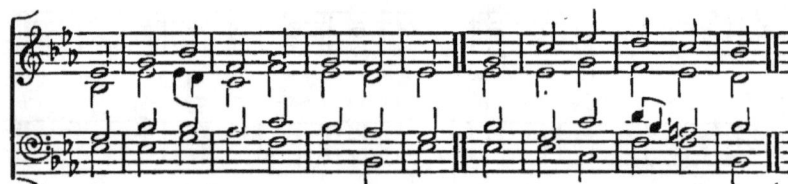

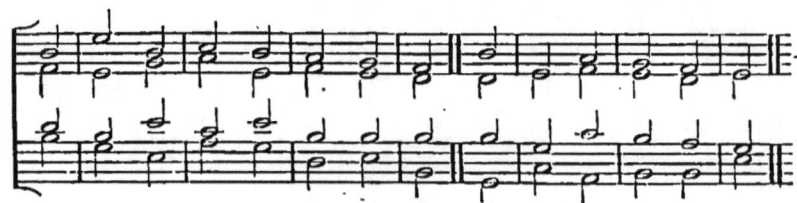

45 *A & m 197* **St. Ann.** c.m.

Denby.

46 **St. Benedict.** c.m.

From Congregational Hymn and Tune Book, by permission.

c

47 327 a & m **St. Bernard.** c.m.

By permission of BURNS and LAMBERT.

48 **St. David.** c.m.

Playford's Psalter, 1671.

(24)

49   **St. Frances.**   c.m.

G. A. Lohr.

50   *300 A ⅄M·*   **St. Magnus.**   c.m.

J. Clark.

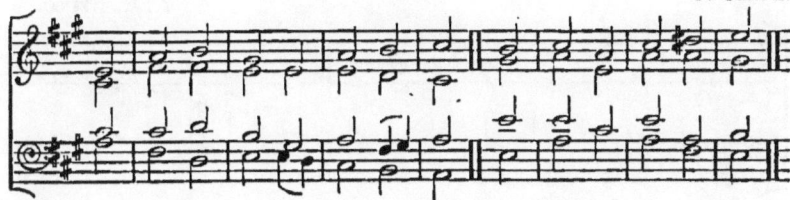

51 𝒶 𝒻 𝓂 80   **St. Mary.**   c.m.

DR. BLOW

52 12 𝒶 𝒻 𝓂   **St. Peter.**   c.m.

A. R. REINAGLE.

(26)

53 _161 a tm_ **St. Stephen.** c.m.

REV. W. JONES.

54 **St. Thomas.** c.m

G. FARNABY, 1592.

55 *62 a+m* **Tallis.** c.m. (Ordination Hymn.)

T. TALLIS.

56 **Tiverton.** c.m.

57   **Tottenham.**   c.m.

58   **Winchester Old.**   c.m.

Alison's Psalter, 1599.

59 *29 a + m*   **Windsor.**   C.M.

G. Kirbye.

60 *475 SPCK*   **York.**   C.M.

Scots Psalter.

61 α ℣m 6   **Angel's Hymn.**   L.M.

ORLANDO GIBBONS.

62   **Arundel.**   L.M.

S. WEBBE.

(31)

63 **Boston.** L.M.

Dr. L. Mason.

64 **British.** L.M.

(32)

Same as Yarmouth p147 Temple Bk

65   **Carey's.** L.M.

66   **Cathedral Chant.** L.M.

The Lord shall come, the earth shall quake,   The mountains to their cen-tre shake;

And with'ring, from the vault of   night,   The stars withdraw their fee-ble   light.

(33)

67   **Charmouth.**   L.M.   E. B. FRIPP

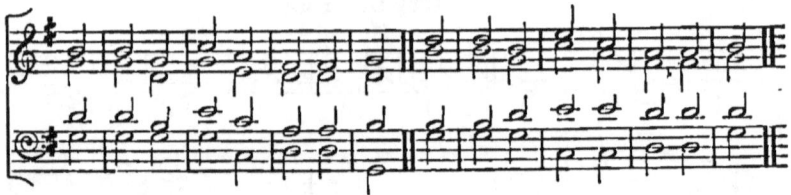

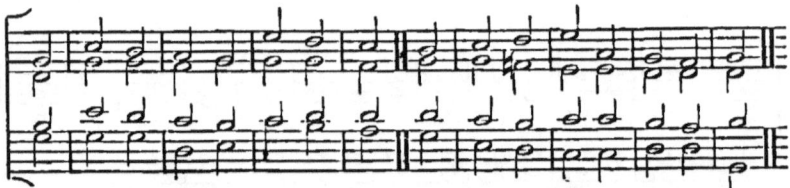

68   **David's Harp.**   L.M.   J. DANIELL.

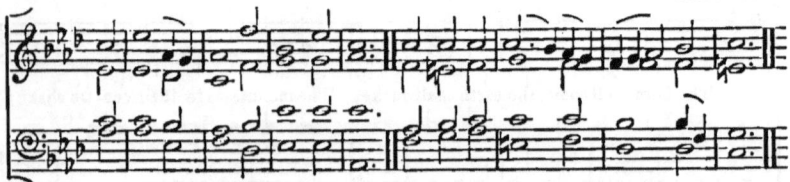

69   **Eden.** L.M.   L. MASON.

70 *Am 23* **Eisenach.** L.M.

J. H. SCHEIN

71   **Ernan.**   L.M.

L. MASON.

72   **Festus.**   L.M.

From a German Chorale.

73   **Gloucester.**   L.M.

DR. HODGES.

74   **Home.**   L.M

From MOZART.

(87)

75 // a 4m **Hursley.** L.M.

Huguenot Melody.

Sun of my soul, Thou Sa-viour dear, It is not night if Thou be near:

O may no earth-born cloud a - rise To hide Thee from Thy ser - vant's eyes.

76 **Lentz.** L.M.

LENTZ.

(38)

77   **Luther's Chant.**   L.M.

78   **Luton.**   L.M.

BURDER.

D

79 *A+m 7 iv* **Magdeburgh.** L.M.

Old "Ten Commandments" Tune.

80 *192 SPCK* **Mainzer.** L.M.

Dr. Mainzer.

(40)

81 A & M 2 **Melcombe.** L.M.

S. WEBBE.

82 **Missionary Chant.** L.M.

(41)

83   **Montgomery.**   L.M.

STANLEY.

84   **Morning Hymn.**   L.M.

BARTHELEMON.

(42)

85   Neapolis.   L.M.

From the Psalmist, by permission.

86   Norfolk.   L.M.

Dr. Howard.
(Altered to Common Time.)

(43)

Nuremberg. L.M.

From Best's Eighty Chorales.

88 *a & m 136* **Old Hundredth.** L.M.

W. FRANC

(44)

88 *136 aƗm* **Old Hundredth.** L.M.

(2nd Arrangement.)

89 **Philadelphia.** L.M.

From the Psalmist, by permission.

90 *Arm 101* **Rockingham.** L.M.

Dr. Millar.

91 **Samson.** L.M.

From Handel.

92 **St. Agnes.** L.M.

A. A. AUSTEN.
By permission of ADDISON and LUCAS.

93 **St. Edward.** L.M.

DR. TURTON.
LORD BISHOP OF ELY.

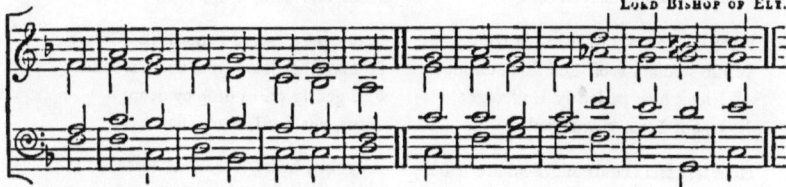

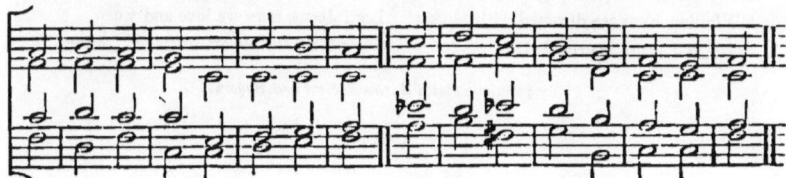

(47)

94 /oo A&M St. Cross. L.M.

Rev. J. B. Dykes.

A-men.

O come and mourn with me awhile ;
O come ye to the Saviour's side ;
O come, together let us mourn ;
Jesus, our Lord, is crucified.

Have we no tears to shed for Him,
While soldiers scoff and Jews deride ?
Ah ! look how patiently He hangs ;
Jesus, our Lord, is crucified.

How fast His Hands and Feet are nail'd ;
His Throat with parching thirst is dried ;
His failing Eyes are dimmed with blood ;
Jesus, our Lord, is crucified.

Seven times He spake, seven words of love ;
And all three hours His silence cried
For mercy on the souls of men ;
Jesus, our Lord, is crucified.

Come, let us stand beneath the Cross ;
So may the Blood from out His Side
Fall gently on us drop by drop·
Jesus, our Lord, is crucified.

A broken heart, a fount of tears
Ask, and they will not be denied ;
Lord Jesus, may we love and weep,
Since Thou for us art crucified.   Amen.

By permission from Hymns Ancient and Modern.

(48)

95 St. Goar. L.M.

96 St. Gregory. L.M.

W. Horsley.

Intercession
A + m 357

St. Luke. L. M.

By permission of Burns and Lambert.

98

St. Olaves. L.M.

HUDSON.

(50)

99 *A & M 10* 𝕿𝖆𝖑𝖑𝖎𝖘' 𝕮𝖆𝖓𝖔𝖓. L.M.

100 *A & M 35* 𝖂𝖎𝖓𝖈𝖍𝖊𝖘𝖙𝖊𝖗. L.M

CRASSELIUS.

(51)

101　　　**Antioch.**　7.7.7.7.

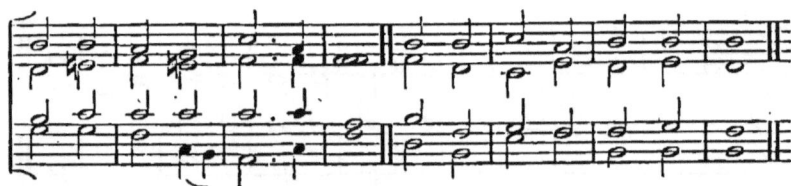

102　　　**Beethoven.**　7.7.7.7.

From BEETHOVEN.

103   **Chester.**   7.7.7.7.

A. Stone.

104   **Christ Chapel.**   7.7.7.7.

Dr. Steggall.

By permission of Addison and Lucas.

105

Eli. 7.7.7.7.

From Costa's *Eli*.
By permission of Addison and Lucas.

106

Ephraim. 7.7.7.7.

Dr. H Leslie.

(51)

107 Geneba. 7.7.7.7.

REV. O. J. LATROBE.

108 SPCK 342 German Hymn. 7.7.7.7

PLEYEL.

(55)

E

109 MS. 32   Crown 178   **Hart's.**   7.7.7.7.

110 A & M 20   **Innocents.**   7.7.7.7.

111   **Latrobe.**   7.7.7.7.

112   **Litany.**   7.7.7.7.

W. WOODWARD.

113 𝒶 ¢ 𝓂 21 **Lubeck.** 7.7.7.7.

German Chorale.

114 **Nottingham.** 7.7.7.7.

From MOZART.

115 *a ⅙m 96* Redhead, No. 47. 7.7.7.7.

R. Redhead.
Original key, C.

116 Sherborne. 7.7.7.7.

From Mendelssohn.

(59)

117   St. Cecilia.   7.7.7.7.   (Prize Tune.)

J. SUMMERS,
Organist of Holy Trinity Church,
Weston-Super-Mare.

118   St. Mark.   7.7.7.7.   (Prize Tune.)

J. ADCOCK, Nottingham.

(60)

119 *A & M 24* **Vienna.** 7.7.7.7.

German Chorale.

120 *233 S. Albans* **Weber.** 7.7.7.7.

From WEBER.

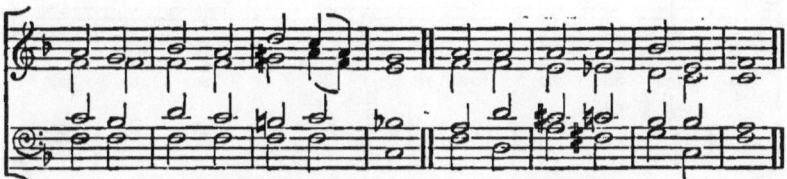

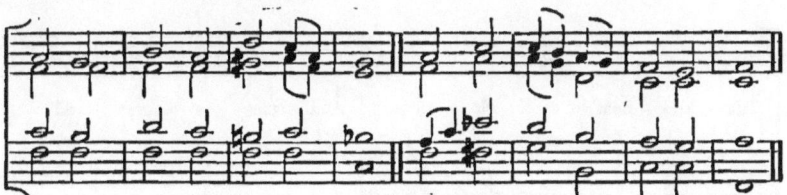

(61)

121 258 a&m **Hanover.**—5.5.5.5.6.5.6.5.

(ii)

Dr. Croft.

Ye ser - vants of God, Your Mas - ter pro - claim,

And pub - lish a - broad His won - der - ful name;

The name all - vic - to - rious Of Je - sus ex - tol;

His king - dom is glo - rious, And rules o - ver all.

Houghton.—5.5.5.5.6.5.6.5.

DR. GAUNTLETT.
From Congregational Psalmist, by permission.

O wor - ship the King All glo - rious a - bove;

O grate - ful - ly sing His power and His love!

Our Shield and De - fen - der, The An - cient of Days,

Pa - vil - ioned in splen - dour, And gird - ed with praise.

Come, let us a - new Our jour - ney pur - sue;

Roll round with the year, And nev - er stand still till the Mas - ter ap - pear.

124   **Hafodwen.**—5.5.8.8.5.5.

Rev. P. Maurice, D.D.

Je - su! guide our way To e - ter - nal day; So shall

we, no more de - lay - ing, Fol - low Thee, Thy voice o -

- bey - ing: Lead us by Thy hand To our Fa - ther's land.

(64)

All ye that pass by, To Je-sus draw nigh, To you is it

no-thing that Je-sus should die? Your ran-som and peace, and

sure-ty He is, Come, see if there e-ver was sor-row like His.

126   **All Saints.**—6.4.6.4.

P. R. SLEEMAN.

To-day the Sa-viour calls, Ye wan-d'rers, home:

O ye be-night-ed souls, Why long-er roam?

Excelsius. 6.4.6.4.6.6.4.

Nearer, my God, to Thee,
    Nearer to Thee;
E'en though it be a cross
    That raiseth me,
Still all my song shall be,
Nearer, my God, to Thee,
    Nearer to Thee!

St. Nicholas. 6.4.6.4.6.6.6.4.

I'm but a stran - ger here, Heaven is my home;

Earth is a de - sert drear, Heaven is my home:

Dan - ger and sor - row stand Round me on eve - ry hand:

Heaven is my Fa - ther - land, Heaven is my home.

Franconia. 6.5.6.5.6.5.6.5.

Why that look of sad - ness? Why that down-cast eye?

Can no thought of glad - ness Lift thy soul on high?

O thou heir of hea - ven, Think of Je - su's love,

While to thee is giv - en All His grace to prove.

130   **Derby.**   6.5,6.5.

Dr. FILITZ's Collection.

Glo - ry   be   to   Je - sus,   Who,   in   bit - ter   pains,

Pour'd   for   me   the   life - blood   From   His   sa - cred   veins.

131   **Harlan.**   6.6.4.6.6.4.

Low-ly and solemn be   Thy children's cry to Thee,   Fa - ther Di - vine!

A hymn of suppliant breath, Own - ing that life and death A - like are Thine.

(69)

Moscow. 6.6.4.6.6.6.4.

GIARDINI.

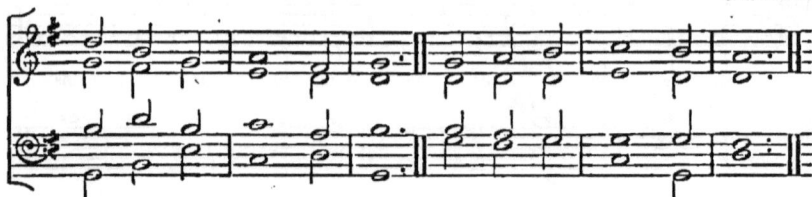

Glory to God on high!
Let heaven and earth reply
Praise ye His name:
Angels, His love adore,
Who all our sorrows bore;
And Saints, cry evermore
Worthy the Lamb!

(70)

133   𝔓𝔥𝔦𝔩𝔦𝔭𝔭𝔦.   6.6.4.6.6.6.4.

J. G. EBELING.

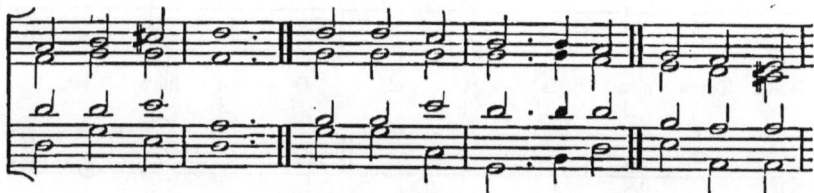

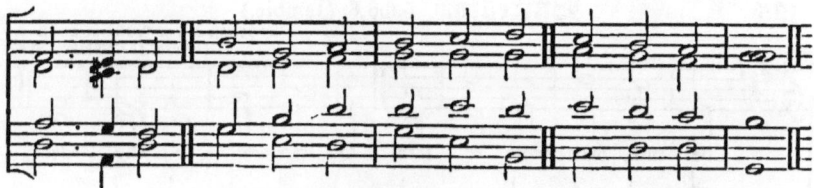

Father of love and power,
Guard Thou our evening hour,
  Shield with Thy might.
For all Thy care this day,
Our grateful thanks we pay,
And to our Father pray,—
  Bless us to-night.

(71.)   F

134 **Miriam.** 6.6.6.4.

J. SUMMERS.

Je - sus Im - man - u - el, Thou shalt our Lead - er be;

Guide Thine own Is - ra - el O - ver life's sea.

135 **Entreaty.** 6.6.6.6. (Iambic.)

By permission of T. Nelson and Sons.
(Altered to Common Time.)

Re - turn, once more re - turn, O wanderer to thy God;

A voice yet on thee calls; A fin - ger points the road.

St. Margaret. 6.6.6.6.6.6.6.6.

Come, breth-ren, ere we part, Bless the Re - deem - er's name;

Join eve - ry tongue and heart, To a - dore and praise the Lamb;

Je - sus, the sin - ner's friend! Him, whom our souls a - dore;

His prais - es have no end; Praise Him for e - ver - more.

St. Bede. 6.6.6.6.7.7.

J. SUMMERS.

Angels, assist to sing
  The honours of your God ;
Touch every tuneful string,
  And sound His name abroad ;
Pour the trembling notes along,
Swell the universal song.

Adoration. 6.6.6.6.8.8.

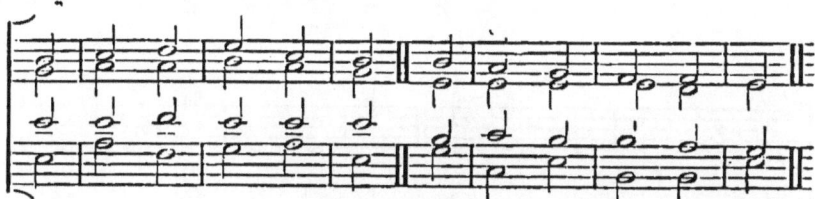

Rejoice, the Lord is King,
Your Lord and King adore,
Mortals, give thanks and sing.
And triumph evermore.
Lift up your hearts, lift up your voice,
Rejoice ; He bids His saints rejoice.

Join all the glorious names
Of wisdom, love and power,
That ever mortals knew,
That angels ever bore:
All are too mean to speak His worth,
Too mean to set my Saviour forth.

(76)

Darwell's 148th. 6.6.6.6.8.8.

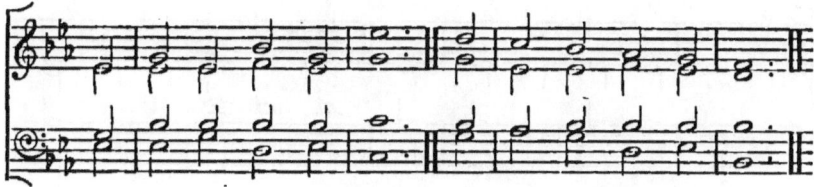

Yes! the Redeemer rose ;
The Saviour left the dead,
And o'er our hellish foes
High raised His conquering head.
　In wild dismay,
　　The guards around
　　Fell to the ground,
　And sank away.

(77)

Old Hundred=and=forty=eighth. 6.6.6.6.8.8.

God is gone up on high.
With a triumphant noise
The clarions of the sky
Proclaim the angelic joys.
Join all on earth, rejoice and sing,
Glory ascribe to glory's King.

St. Swithin. 6.6.6.6.8.8.

JESSER.

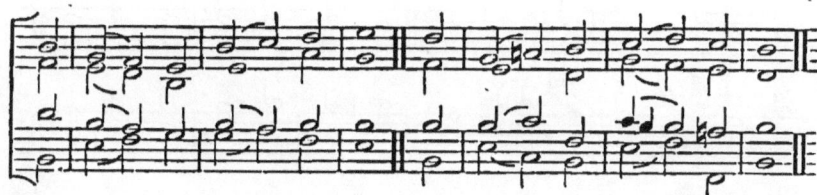

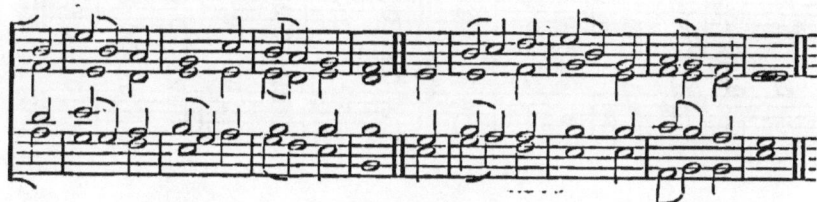

O Heaven, abode of saints,
  Where sin can never come,
For Thee my spirit faints;
  I long to be at home.
O world of peace, O land of rest,
When shall I reach thee and be blessed?

Fulneck. 6.6.7.7.7.7.

Rev. C. J. La Trobe.
(Altered to Common time.)

Worthy, O Lord, art Thou,
That ev'ry knee should bow,
Ev'ry tongue to Thee confess;
Universal nature join,
Strong and mighty Thee to bless,
Gracious, merciful, benign.

Leoni. 6.6.8.4.6.6.8.4.

Hebrew Melody. Harmony by M. Costa.

By permission of Addison and Lucas, 210, Regent Street.

The God of A-br'am praise, Who reigns en-thron'd a-bove;

An-tient of ev-er-last-ing days, And God of Love!

Je-ho-vah, great I AM! By earth and heav'n con-fess'd;

I bow and bless the sa-cred name, For e-ver bless'd.

Bach. D.S.M.

German Chorale
Harmonized by J. S. Bach

Thou art gone up on high, To realms be - yond the skies;

And round Thy throne un - ceas-ing - ly The songs of praise a - rise;

But we are ling-'ring here, With sin and care op - pressed:

Lord, send Thy pro-mised Com-fort - er, And lead us to our rest.

Fairfield. D.S.M.

Rev. P. La Trobe.

Give to the winds thy fears; Hope, and be un-dis-mayed;

God hears thy sighs and counts thy tears, God shall lift up thy head.

Thro' waves, and clouds, and storms, He gent-ly clears thy way:

Wait thou His time, so shall the night Soon end in joy-ous day.

Ascalon. 6.6.8.6.6.8.

From the Congregational Psalmist, by permission.

How pleased and blest was I
To hear the people cry,—
Come, let us seek our God to-day !
Yes, with a cheerful zeal
We haste to Sion's hill,
And thère our vows and homage pay.

(84)

St. Vincent. 6.6.8.6.8.7.

A STONE.

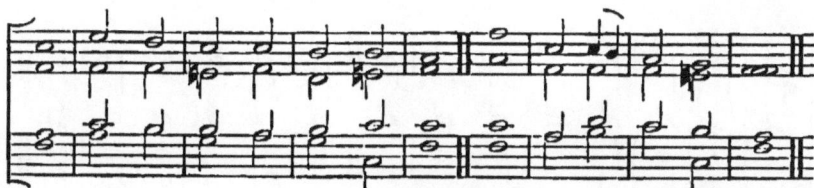

From Egypt's bondage come,
Where death and darkness reign.
We seek our new, our better home,
Where we our rest shall gain.
Alleluia!   Alleluia!
We are on our way to God.

(85)

149 **𝔏ucca.** 6.6.8.6.8.8.

J. H. Schein.

Friend after friend departs,
Who hath not lost a friend?
There is no union here of hearts,
That finds not here an end.
Were this frail world our final rest,
Living or dying, none were blest.

(86)

150 𝕰𝕝𝕓𝕖𝕪. 6.6.10.6.6.10.

Dr. G. J. Elvey.

Thou who didst stoop be - low To drain the cup of woe,

And wear the form of frail mor - tal - i - - ty;

Thy bless - ed la - bors done, Thy crown of vic - t'ry won,

Hast pass'd from earth, pass'd to Thy home on high.

(87) G

Wittemburg. 6.7.6.7.6.6.6.6.

J. CRUGER.

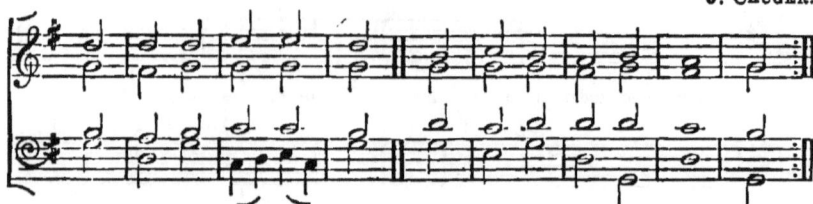

Let all men praise the Lord,
In worship lowly bending;
On His most holy word,
Redeemed from woe, depending,
He gracious is, and just,
From childhood us doth lead;
On Him we place our trust
And hope, in time of need.

Glory and praise to God,
To Father, Son, be given,
And to the Holy Ghost,
On high enthron'd in Heaven.
Praise to the Triune God;
With powerful arm and strong,
He changeth night to day;
Praise Him in grateful song.

152 **Halifax.** 6.8.6.4.

From Congregational Church Music, by permission.

Lo, on th'inglorious tree, The Lord, the Lord of glo - ry hangs;

For - sa - ken now is He, And pierc'd with pangs.

153 **Homburg.** 6.10.6.10.

A. R. REINAGLE.

Birds have their qui - et nests, Fox - es their holes, and man his peace - ful bed;

All creatures have their rest, But Je - sus had not where to lay His head.

(89)

154   **Easter Hymn.**   7.4.7.4.7.4.7.4.

HENRY CAREY.

Easter Hymn. 7.4.7.4.7.4.7.4.

W. H. MONK.

Al - le - lu - ia.

Al - le - lu - ia.

Al - le - lu - ia.

Al - le - lu - ia.

156   **St. Alphege.**   7.6.7.6.

Dr. Gauntlett.

From Church Hymn and Tune Book, by permission

157   **St. Philip.**   7.6.7.6.

A. Stone.

Brief life is here our por - tion; Brief sor - row, short-liv'd care:

The life that knows no end - ing, The tear - less life, is *there.*

St. Alban's. 7.6.7.6.7.6.7.6.

GRAUN.

O sacred Head, once wounded,
   With grief and pain weighed down
How scornfully surrounded
   With thorns, Thine only crown!
How pale art Thou with anguish,
   With sore abuse and scorn!
How does that visage languish,
   Which once was bright as morn!

(93)

Ewing. 7.6.7.6.7.6.7.6.

A. Ewing.

Je - ru - sa - lem the gol -den,   With milk and ho - ney blest;

Be - neath thy con - tem - pla - tion   Sink heart and voice op - prest:

I know not, Oh I know not,   What joys a - wait us   there;

What ra - dian - cy of glo - ry,   What bliss be - yond com - pare!

160 **Missionary.** 7.6.7.6.7.6.7.6.

Dr. L. Mason.

Some - times a light sur - pris - es The Chris - tian while he sings:

It is the Lord, who ri - ses With heal - ing in His wings.

When com - forts are de - clin - ing, He grants the soul a - gain

A sea - son of clear shin - ing, To cheer it af - ter rain.

(95)

Munich. 7.6.7.6.7.6.7.6.

German Melody, 1648.

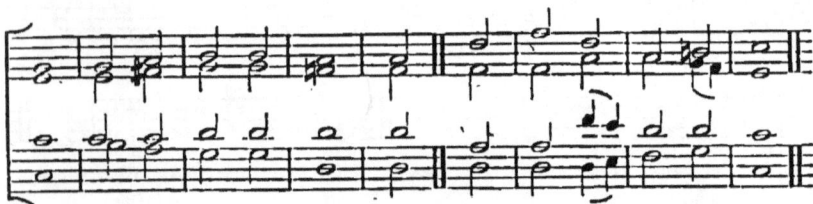

For thee, O dear, dear Country
Mine eyes their vigils keep;
For very love, beholding
Thy happy name, they weep.
The mention of thy glory
Is unction to the breast,
And medicine in sickness,
And love, and life, and rest.

162   St. Theodulph.   7.6.7.6.7.6.7.6.

MELCHIOR TESCHNER, 1613.

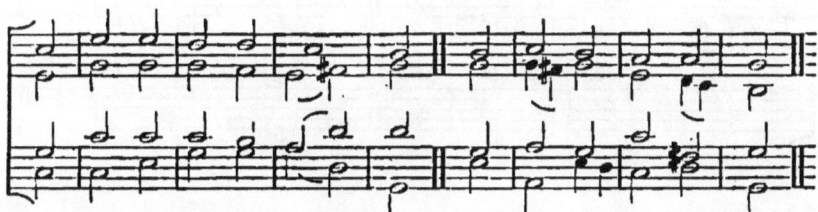

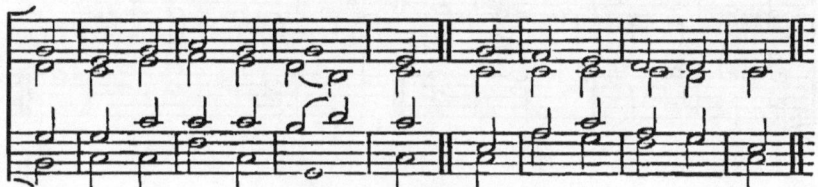

From Greenland's icy mountains,
From India's coral strand,
Where Afric's sunny fountains
Roll down their golden sand ;
From many an ancient river,
From many a palmy plain,
They call us to deliver
Their land from error's chain.

Holywell. 7.6.7.6.7.7.

A. R. REINAGLE.

Not Thy garment's hem alone,
  My trembling faith would hold.
Though Divine compassion shone
  Beneath its sacred fold :—
Thou didst own her mute appeal,
Who besought Thy power to heal.

164

St. Saviour's. 7.6.7.6.7.7.

From·MENDELSSOHN.

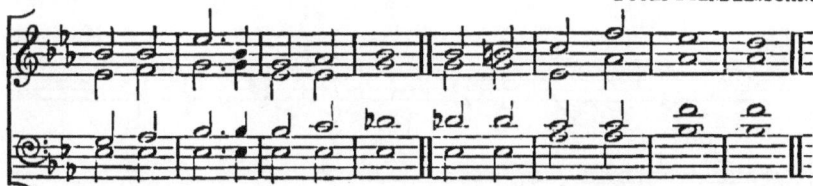

In the day of thy distress,
  May Jehovah hear thee !
In the hour when dangers press,
  Jacob's God be near thee !
Send thee from His holy place,
'Timely aid, or strengthening grace !

May thy prayers and offerings rise,
  By thy God recorded !
Thine oblations reach the skies,
  Graciously rewarded !
Granted be thy heart's request ;
All thy purposes be blest.

Thy success our hearts shall cheer,
  We with exultation
In Jehovah's name will rear
  Trophies of salvation.
Go beneath His guardian care.
And the Lord fulfil thy prayer.

165   **Chesterfield.**   7.6.7.6.7.7.7.6.

Moravian.

Meet and right it is to sing,
At every time and place,
Glory to our heavenly King,
The God of truth and grace:
Join we then with sweet accord,
All in one thanksgiving join:
Holy, Holy, Holy Lord!
Eternal praise be thine.

(100)

St. Hilary 7.6.7.6.7.7.7.6.

Rev. J. B. DYKES.

Rise, my soul, and stretch thy wings, Thy bet - ter por - tion trace;

Rise from tran - si - to - ry things Tow'rds heav'n, thy na - tive place.

Sun and moon and stars de-cay, Time shall soon this earth re-move,

Rise, my soul, and haste a - way, To seats pre-pared a - bove.

Atonement. 7.6.7.6.7.8.7.6.

Lamb of God, Whose bleed-ing love We now re-call to mind,

Send the an-swer from a-bove, And let us mer-cy find;

Think on us who think on Thee, And ev'-ry struggling soul re-lease;

O re-mem-ber Cal-va-ry, And bid us go in peace.

Russell Place. 7.6.7.6.7.6.7.8.7.6.

W. STERNDALE BENNETT.

Praise the Lord who reigns a - bove, And keeps His courts be - low;

Praise Him for His bound-less love, And all His great - ness shew;

Praise Him for His no - ble deeds; O praise Him for His matchless power:

Him, from whom all good pro - ceeds, Let earth and heaven a - dore.

169 **Capetown.** 7.7.7.5.

FILITZ.

170 **Ledbury.** 7.7.7.5.

A. KING.

Lord of mer - cy and of might, Of man - kind the life and light,

Rall.

Ma - ker, Teach - er, In - fi - nite; Je - sus, hear and save!

(104)

Bethany. 7.7.7.7.7.7

Moravian.

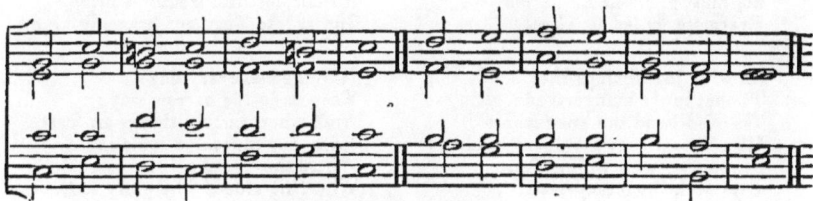

God of mercy, god of grace,
Shew the brightness of Thy Face;
Shine upon us, Saviour, shine.
Fill Thy Church with light divine;
And Thy saving health extend
Unto earth's remotest end.

Dix. 7.7.7.7.7.7.

As with gladness men of old
Did the guiding star behold;
As with joy they hailed its light,
Leading onward, beaming bright;
So, most gracious Lord, may we
Evermore be led to Thee.

As with joyful steps they sped
To that lowly manger-bed:
There to bend the knee before
Him Whom heav'n and earth adore;
So may we with willing feet
Ever seek the mercy-seat.

As they offered gifts most rare
At that manger rude and bare;
So may we with holy joy,
Pure and free from sins alloy,
All our costliest treasures bring,
Christ! to Thee our heavenly king.

Holy Jesus, every day
Keep us in the narrow way;
And, when earthly things are past,
Bring our ransomed souls at last
Where they need no star to guide,
Where no clouds Thy glory hide.

In the heavenly country bright
Need they no created light;
Thou its Light, its Joy, its Crown,
Thou its Sun which goes not down:
There for ever may we sing
Alleluias to our King.

Nassau. 7.7.7.7.7.7.

J. ROSENMULLER.

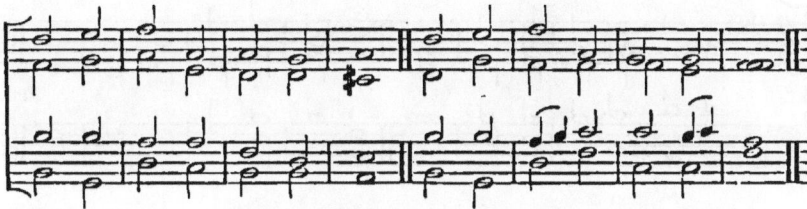

Christ, Whose glory fills the skies,
Christ, the true, the only Light,
Sun of Righteousness, arise,
Triumph o'er the shades of night;
Dayspring from on high be near,
Daystar in my heart appear.

(107)

174 𝕮𝖆𝖘𝖘𝖊𝖑. 7.7.7.7.7.7.

By permission of T. Nelson and Sons.

Fine.

D.C.

175 𝕾𝖕𝖆𝖎𝖓. 7.7.7.7.7.7.

Fine.

D.C.

(108)

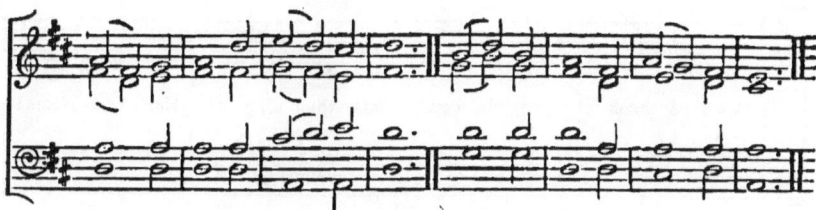

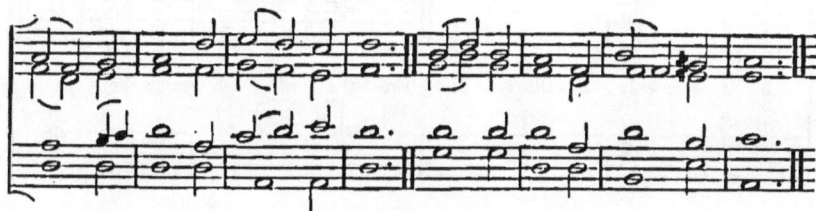

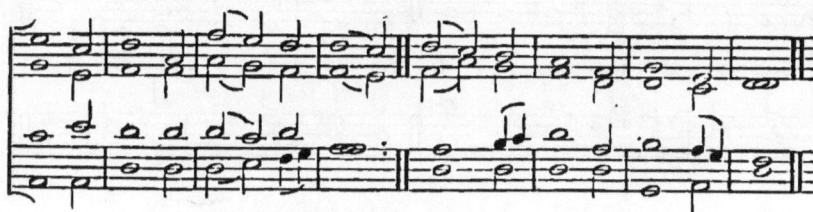

Rock of ages, cleft for me,
Let me hide myself in Thee;
Let the Water and the Blood,
From Thy wounded Side which flowed,
Be of sin the double cure,
Save from wrath and make me pure.

(109)

177   **Coburg.**   7.7.7.7.7.7.7.7.

H.R.H. the late PRINCE CONSORT.

Come, ye thank-ful peo - ple, come, Raise the song of Har - vest-Home!

All is safe - ly 'ga - ther'd in, . Ere the win - ter storms be - gin;

God, our Ma - ker, doth pro - vide For our wants to be sup - plied;

Come to God's own tem - ple, come; Raise the song of Har - vest-Home!

(110)

178 Christmas Hymn

MENDELSSOHN.

Hark! the he-rald-an-gels sing Glo-ry to the new-born King, Peace on earth, and mer-cy mild, God and sin-ners re-con-ciled. Joy-ful, all ye na-tions, rise, Join the triumph of the skies; With th' an-ge-lic host proclaim Christ is born in Beth-le-hem. Hark! the he-rald an-gels sing Glo-ry to the new-born King.

Organ Pedal.

(111)

Refuge. 7.7.7.7.7.7.7.7.

J. SUMMERS.

Je - sus, Re-fuge of my soul, Let me to Thy bo - som fly,

While the near - er wa - ters roll, While the tem - pest still is high;

Hide me, O my Sa - viour! hide, Till the storm of life be past;

Safe in - to the ha - ven guide, O re - ceive my soul at last!

Syria 7.7.7.7.7.7.7.7.

Ho - ly, Ho - ly, Ho - ly Lord God of Hosts, when heaven and earth

Out of dark - ness, at Thy word, Is - sued in - to glo - rious birth:

All Thy works a - round Thee stood, And Thine eye be - held them good,

While they sang with sweet ac - cord, Ho - ly, Ho - ly, Ho - ly Lord.

(113)

181　　　**Tichfield.**　7.7.7.7.7.7.7.7.

From "Crown of Jesus" Music.
By permission.

Sa - viour, when in dust to Thee Low we bow th' a - dor-ing knee;

When, re - pent - ant, to the skies Scarce we lift our weep - ing eyes,

Oh, by all Thy pains and woe Suf - fered once for man be - low,

Bend - ing from Thy throne on high, Hear our so - lemn li - ta - ny.

(114)

182 **Peter's Hill.** 7.7.7.7.8.7.

R. A. FIRTH.

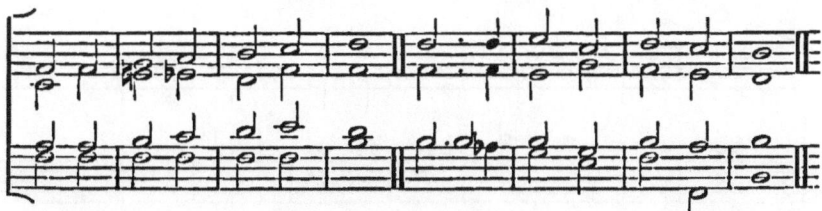

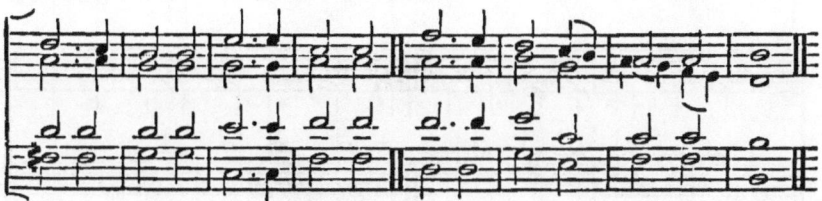

Thou who didst for Peter's faith
Kindly condescend to pray!
Thou whose loving kindness hath
Kept me to the present day!
  Kind Conductor,
Still direct my devious way.

183 **Glentworth.** 7.7.7.7.8.8.

J. SUMMERS.

Onward let my children go,
God the Lord commands us so ;
Though the path be through the sea,
Little flock, what's that to thee?
Only trust His love unbounded,
Thou shalt never be confounded.

Florence. 7.7.7.8.8.8.

A. R. Reinagle.

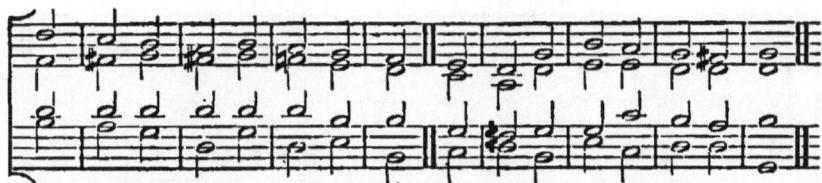

Lord, we raise our cry to Thee,
Like the blind beside the way ;
Make our darken'd souls to see
The glory of Thy perfect day ;
O Lord, rebuke our sullen night,
And give Thyself unto our sight.

185 **Lostwithiel.** 7.7.8.7.7.7.8.7.

J. TURLE.

Head of the Church tri-um-phant, We joy-ful-ly a-dore Thee;

Till Thou ap-pear, Thy mem-bers here Shall sing like those in glo-ry;

We lift our hearts and voi-ces, With blest an-ti-ci-pa-tion;

And cry a-loud, and give to God The praise of our sal-va-tion.

186   **Mercy.**   7.8.7.8.

Je - sus lives! no lon - ger now Can thy terrors, Death, ap - pal us; Je - sus

lives! and this we know, Thou, O Grave, canst not en - thral us.   Al - le - lu - ia.

187   **Knowlton.**   7.8.7.8.

DR. GAUNTLETT.

Fear no more the clanking chain; Thou'rt free as the light of hea - ven;

For stripes, and wea - ri - ness, and pain, The eter - nal rest is gi - ven;

(119)   I

Braine, No. 22. 8.4.8.4.8.8.8.4.

God, who madest earth and heaven,
    Darkness and light;
Who the day for toil hath given,
    For rest the night;
May Thine angel-guards defend us,
Slumber sweet Thy mercy send us,
Holy dreams and hopes attend us,
    This live-long night.

Guard us waking, guard us sleeping,
    And, when we die,
May we in Thy mighty keeping
    All peaceful lie:
When the last dread call shall wake us,
Do not Thou our God forsake us,
But to reign in glory take us
    With Thee on high.

189   **St. Cuthbert.**   8.6.8.4.

Rev. J. B. DYKES.

Our blest Redeemer, ere He breathed
  His tender last farewell,
A Guide, a Comforter, bequeathed
  With us to dwell.

He comes, sweet influence to impart,
  A gracious willing Guest,
Where He can find one humble heart,
  Wherein to rest.

And His that gentle voice we hear,
  Soft as the breath of even,   [fear,
That checks each thought, that calms each
  And speaks of heaven.

And every virtue we possess,
  And every victory won,
And every thought of holiness,
  Are His alone.

Spirit of purity and grace,
  Our weakness, pitying, see;
O make our hearts Thy dwelling-place,
  And worthier Thee.

O praise the Father, praise the Son;
  Blest Spirit, praise to Thee;
All praise to God, the Three in One,
  The One in Three.

By permission, from *Hymns Ancient and Modern*.

Allhallows. 8.6.8.6.8.6.

A. H. Brown.

Beyond, beyond that boundless sea,
Above that dome of sky,
Farther than thought itself can flee,
Thy dwelling is on high;
Yet dear the awful thought to me,
That Thou, my God, art nigh.

Spohr. 8.6.8.6.8.6., (or c.m. omitting * to *.)

From Spohr.

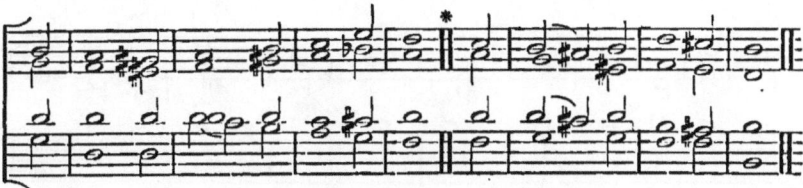

For ever will I bless the Lord,
Nor cease His praise to speak;
My song His goodness shall record,
That the oppressed and weak
May trust in Him, who will reward
The humble and the meek.

(123)

St. Matthew. D.C.M.

Dr. Croft

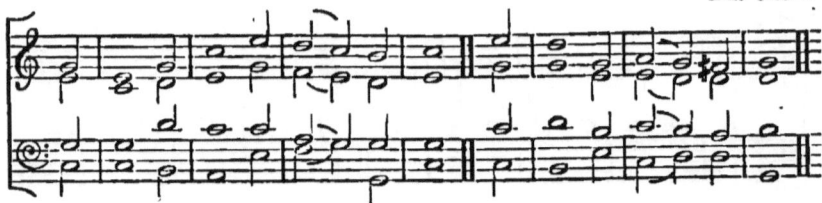

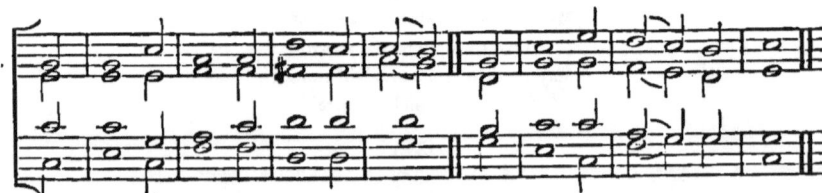

Usk. D.C.M.

English Psalter, 1562.

When as we sat in Ba - by - lon, The ri - vers round a - bout,

And in re - mem-brance of Si - on, The tears for grief burst out ;—

We hanged our harps and in - stru-ments The wil - low trees up - on;

For in that place men for their use Had plant - ed ma - ny one.

194   **Brunswick.**   8.6.8.6.8.8.   From HANDEL.

𝔓𝔞𝔩𝔪𝔶𝔯𝔞. 8.6.8.6.8.8.

J. SUMMERS.

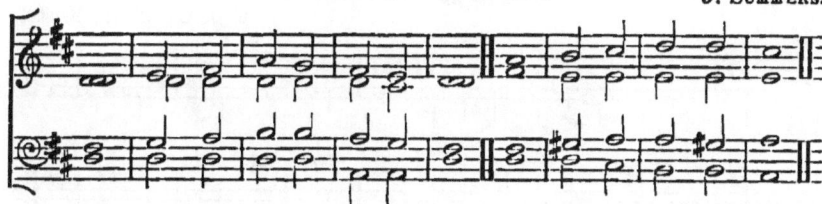

Thou art the Everlasting Word,
　The Father's only Son;
God, manifestly seen and heard,
　And Heaven's beloved One.
Worthy, O Lamb of God, art Thou,
That every knee to Thee should bow.

196 **Royal Fort.** 8.6.8.8.6.

E. J. Orchard, Bristol

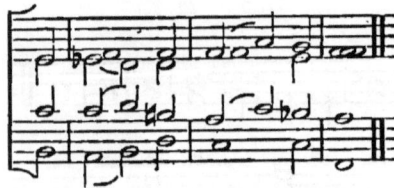

Eternal Light! Eternal Light!
  How pure the soul must be, [sight,
When, placed within Thy searching
It shrinks not, but with calm delight
  Can live and look on Thee.

197 **Hulme.** 8.6.6.

J. C. Ebeling.

Ere I sleep, for every favor,
This day shewed by my God,
I will bless my Saviour.

198   **Batabia.**   8.7.8.7.

German.

199   **Canterbury.**   8.7.8.7.

Rev. C. J. La Trobe.

HMS 389

200 (29 Bateman) **Mariners'.** 8.7.8.7.

201 **Pange lingua,** 8.7.8.7.

Ancient Latin Hymn.

202   **Sardis.**   8.7.8.7.

From BEETHOVEN.

203   **Sharon.**   8.7.8.7.

Dr. BOYCE.

204   **St. Oswald.**   8.7.8.7.

Rev. J. B. DYKES.

205   **Solicitude.**   8.7.8.7.7.7.

J. DANIELL, Bristol.

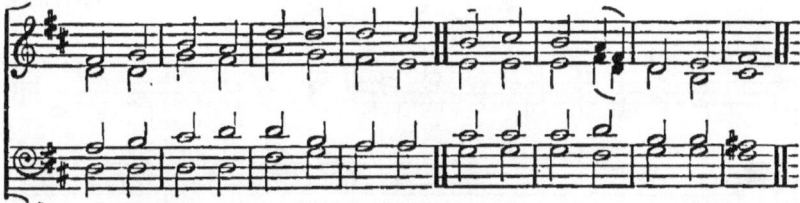

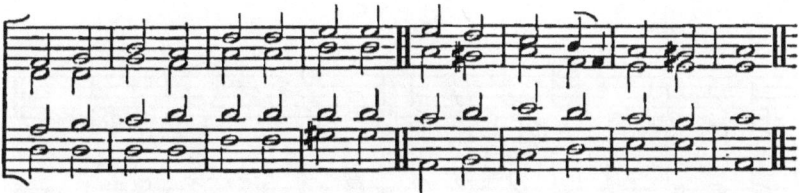

𝕰𝖇𝖊𝖓𝖘𝖔𝖓𝖌. 8.7.8.7.7.7

J. SUMMERS.

Through the day Thy love has spared us,
Now we lay us down to rest;
Through the silent watches guard us,
Let no foe our peace molest;
Jesu, Thou our guardian be;
Sweet it is to trust in Thee. .

Pilgrims here on earth, and strangers,
Dwelling in the midst of foes,
Us and ours preserve from dangers,
In Thine Arms may we repose,
And, when life's sad day is past,
Rest with Thee in heaven at last.

207 *52 a rm* **Benediction.**   8.7.8.7.8.7.

S. WEBBE.

Dismissal. 8.7.8.7.8.7.

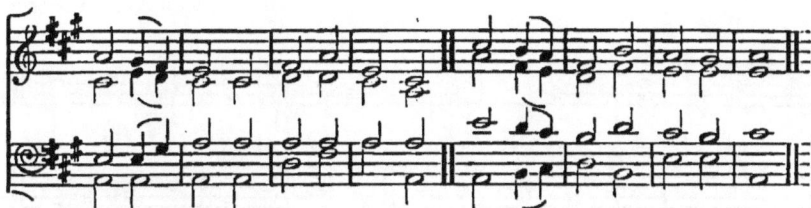

K

209   𝔙ogler.   8.7.8.7.8.7.

The Abbè VOGLER.

210 *39 a & m* **St. Werburgh.** 8.7.8.7.8.7.

S. WEBBE

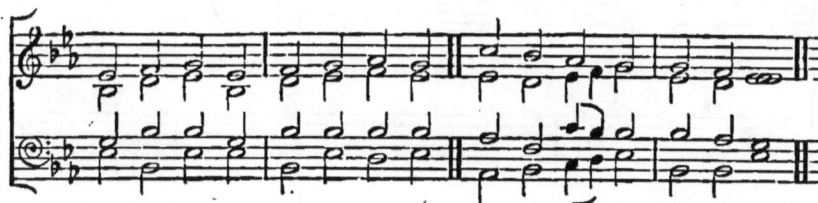

211 **Zurich.** 8.7.8.7.8.7.
or 7.7.

J. SCHOP, 1640.

What is life? 'tis but a va-pour, Soon it van-ish-es a-way:

Life is like a dy-ing ta-per; O, my soul, why wish to stay?

Why not spread thy wings and fly . . Straight to yon-der world of joy?

212 **Hanover Palace.** 8.7.8.7.7.7.4.4.7.7.

His Majesty GEORGE V.,
King of Hanover.

Lord, vouchsafe us Thy pro-tec-tion, As we leave Thy house of pray'r;

(138)

Grant us Thy di - vine di - rec - tion, Thro' a world of sin and care; Ma - ny foes be - set our way, As we jour - ney day by day: By pos - sess - ing Thy good bless - ing, We shall reach the heav'n - ly shore, Where temp - ta - tions vex no more.

Granta. 8.7.8.7.8.7.8.7.

Dr. T. A. Walmisley

Come, Thou long - ex - péct - ed Je - sus, Born to set Thy peo - ple free;

From our fears and sins re - lease us: Let us find our rest in Thee.

Is - rael's strength and con - so - la - tion, Hope of all the earth Thou art:

Dear de - sire of eve - ry na - tion, Joy of eve - ry long - ing heart.

Tantum ergo. 8.7.8.7.8.7.8.7.

V. NOVELLO.

215 *SPCK 491* **Vesper.** 8.7.8.7.8.7.8.7.

(142)

Stanmore. 8.7.8.7.6.6.8.8.

A. GILBERT.

I lay me down in peace to sleep, To Thee I would com - mend me;

I trust my Guard - ian Thou wilt keep, And in this night de - fend me:

Of death I'm not a - fraid, Nor world, nor hell I dread;

For who with Je - sus shuts his eyes, He al - so shall with Je - sus rise.

(143)

Luther's Hymn. 8.7.8.7.8.8.7. (Correctly, 8.8.8.8.8.8.)

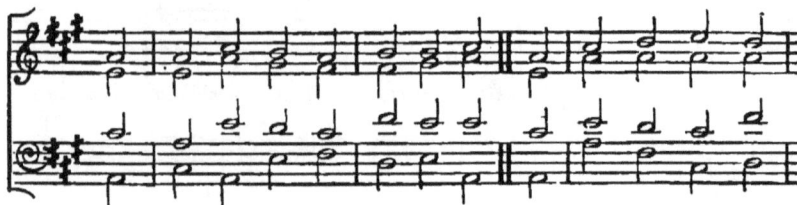

Great God, what do we see and hear!
The end of things created!
The Judge of mankind doth appear,
On clouds of glory seated;
The trumpet sounds, the graves restore
The dead whom they contained before:
Prepare, my soul, to meet Him.

Zoheleth. 8.7.8.7.8.8.7.

Rev. W. H. Havergal.

The Lord of might from Si - nai's brow Gave forth His voice of

thun - der; And Is - rael lay on earth be - low, Out-stretch'd in

fear and won - der; Be - neath His feet was pitch - y night,

And at His left hand and His right The rocks were rent a - sun - der.

(145)

Drayton. 8.8.6.8.8.6.

Moravian.

O Lord, how happy should we be,
If we could cast our care on Thee,
  If we from self could rest;
And feel, at heart, that One above,
In perfect wisdom, perfect love,
  Is working for the best!

Inspruck. 8.8,6.8.8.6.

German Chorale.

Harmony by C. H. RINK.

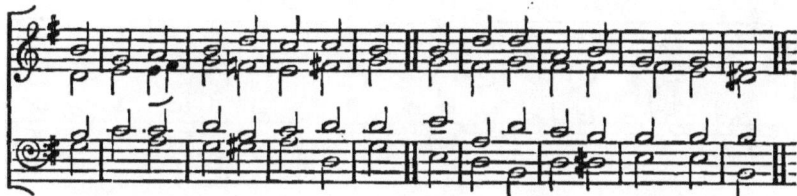

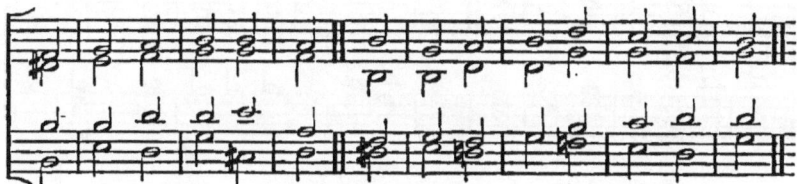

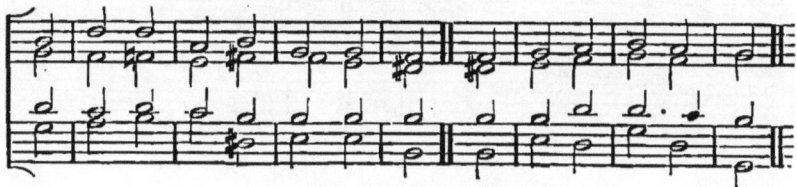

That Thou, O Lord, art ever nigh,
Though veiled in awful majesty,
 Thy mighty works declare;
Thy hand this earthly frame upholds,
Thine eye the universe beholds
 With providential care.

Pembroke. 8.8.6.8.8.6.

J. FOSTER, Bristol.

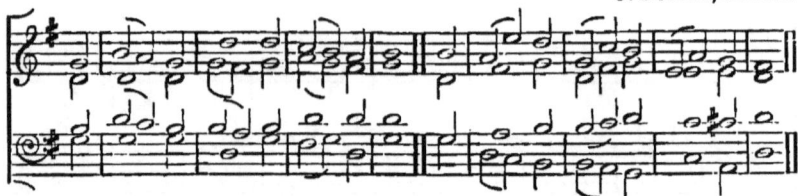

There is a Dwelling-place above ;—
Thither, to meet the God of love,
    The poor in spirit go ;
There is a Paradise of rest ;—
For contrite hearts and souls distrest
    Its streams of comfort flow.

222 **Stabat mater.** 8.8.7.

At the Cross her sta - tion keep - ing, Stood the mourn-ful

Mo - ther weep - ing, Where He hung, the dy - ing Lord;

223 **Winter.** 8.8.7.

From WINTER.

224 **Rink.** 8.9.7.8.8.7.8.8.8.

German Chorale.
Harmony by C. H. RINK.

Behold how glorious is yon sky;
Lo! there the righteous never die,
But dwell in peace for ever;
Then who would wear this earthly clay,
When bid to cast life's chains away,
And win Thy gracious favour?
Holy, Holy, O forgive us,
And receive us, Heavenly Father,
When around Thy throne we gather.

Confiding in Thy sacred word,
Our Saviour is our hope, O Lord,
The guiding Star before us;
Our Shepherd leading us the way,
If from Thy paths our footsteps stray,
To Thee He will restore us:
Holy, Holy, ever hear us,
And receive us, while we gather
Round Thy throne, Almighty Father.

(150)

St. Aidan. 8.8.8. (Iambic.)

Hon. and Rev. F. R. Grey.

Arranged by Rev. J. B. Dykes.

O God of life, Whose pow'r be - nign Doth o'er the
world in mer - cy shine, Ac - cept our praise, for we are Thine.

Abignon. 8.8.8.6.

Triller, 1559.

Lo, the storms of life are breaking, Faithless fears our hearts are shaking,
For our suc-cour un-der - ta-king, Lord and Sa-viour, help us.

L

Dies Iræ. (8.8.8. Trochaic.)

ARTHUR HENRY BROWN,
Organist of Brentwood, Essex.

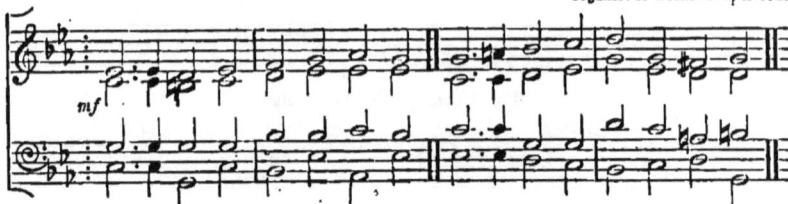

DAY of Wrath! O day of mourning!
See fulfilled the prophet's warning!
Heaven and earth in ashes burning!

Oh, what fear man's bosom rendeth,
When from heaven the Judge descendeth,
On Whose sentence all dependeth!

Wondrous sound the trumpet flingeth,
Through earth's sepulchres it ringeth,
All before the Throne it bringeth.

Death is struck, and nature quaking,
All creation is awaking,
To its Judge an answer making.

Lo, the Book, exactly worded,
Wherein all hath been recorded!
Thence shall judgment be awarded.

When the Judge His seat attaineth,
And each hidden deed arraigneth,
Nothing unavenged remaineth.

What shall I, frail man, be pleading,
Who for me be interceding,
When the just are mercy needing?

King of Majesty tremendous,
Who dost free salvation send us,
Fount of pity, then befriend us!

Think, good JESU, my salvation
Caused Thy wondrous Incarnation;
Leave me not to reprobation.

Faint and weary Thou hast sought me,
On the Cross of suffering bought me;
Shall such grace be vainly brought me?

(152)

Righteous Judge! for sin's pollution
Grant Thy gift of absolution,
Ere that day of retribution.

Guilty, now I pour my moaning,
All my shame with anguish owning;
Spare, O GOD, Thy suppliant groaning.

Thou the sinful woman savedst;
Thou the dying thief forgavest;
And to me a hope vouchsafest.

Worthless are my prayers and sighing,
Yet, good LORD, in grace complying,
Rescue me from fires undying.

With Thy favoured sheep O place me,
Nor among the goats abase me;
But to Thy right hand upraise me.

While the wicked are confounded,
Doomed to flames of woe unbounded,
Call me, with Thy saints surrounded.

Low I kneel, with heart-submission
See, like ashes, my contrition;
Help me in my last condition.

cres - - - cen - - - - do.

V. 18. Ah! that day of tears and mourn-ing! From the dust of earth re-turn-ing,

Man for judg-ment must pre-pare him; Spare, O God, in mer-cy spare him!

Lord all pity-ing, Je-su blest, Grant him Thine e-ter-nal rest. A - men.

(153)

228 **St. Fabian.** 8.8.8.6.

J. Summers.

Just as I am, with-out one plea, But that Thy blood was shed for me,

And that Thou bid'st me come to Thee— O, Lamb of God, I come.

229 **Silberstone.** 8.9.8.6.

T. M. Mudie.

O, ho-ly Sa-viour, Friend un-seen, Since on Thine arm Thou bid'st us lean;

Help me, throughout life's changing scene, By faith to cling to Thee.

230   **David.**   8.8.8.8.

From Handel.

231   **Doncaster.**   8.8.8.8.

Adapted from Dr. Miller.

In - spi - rer and Hearor of Pray'r, Thou Shepherd and Guardian of Thine,

My all to Thy co - ve-nant care, I, sleeping and wa - king, re - sign.

(155)

Oberlin. 8.8.8.8.6.

DR. S. ELVEY.

O Lord, Thy heavenly grace impart,
And fix my frail inconstant heart ;
Henceforth my chief desire shall be
To dedicate myself to Thee;
To Thee, my God, to Thee.

Hosanna. 8.8.8.8.7.

Ho - san - na to the Liv - ing Lord! Ho - san - na to th' In
- car - nate Word! To Christ, Cre - a - tor, Sa - viour, King, Let
earth, let heav'n, Ho-san - na sing, Ho - san - na in the high - est!

Hosanna, Lord! Thine angels cry;
Hosanna, Lord! Thy saints reply:
Above, beneath us, all around,
The dead, the living, swell the sound,
　　Hosanna in the highest!

O Saviour, with protecting care,
Return to this Thy house of prayer;
Assembled in Thy sacred name,
Here we Thy parting promise claim.
　　Hosanna in the highest!

But chiefest, in our cleansèd breast,
Eternal! bid Thy Spirit rest;
And make our secret soul to be
A temple pure, and worthy Thee.
　　Hosanna in the highest!

So, in the last and dreadful day,
When earth and heaven shall melt away,
Thy flock, redeemed from sinful stain,
Shall swell the sound of praise again.
　　Hosanna in the highest!

234 **Worms.** 8.8.8.8.6.6.6.6.8.

M. Luther.

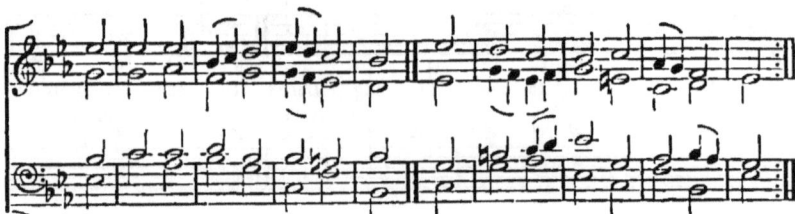

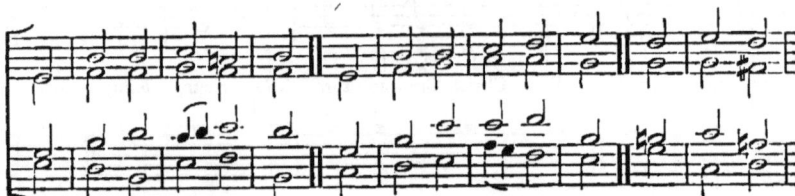

God is our refuge in distress,
Our shield of hope through every care;
Our helper, watching us to bless,
And therefore will we not despair,
   Although the mountains shake,
   And hills their place forsake,
   And waters o'er them break,
  Yet still we will not fear,
For Thou O God, art ever near.

God is our hope and strength in woe,
Through earth he maketh wars to cease,
His power breaketh spear and bow,
His mercy sendeth endless peace.
   Then though the earth remove,
   And storms rage high above,
   And seas tempestuous prove,
  Yet still we will not fear,
The Lord of Hosts is ever near.

Eaton. 8.8. 8.8. 8.8.

Wyvill.

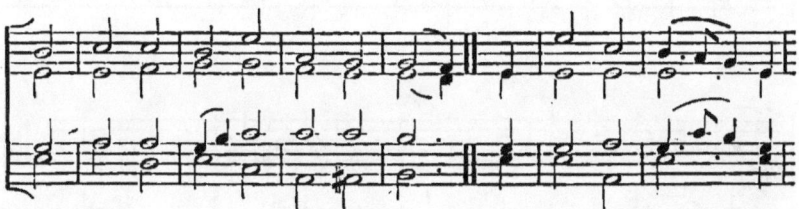

236   **Halle.**   8.8. 8.8. 8.8.

H. KUGELMANN, 1540.

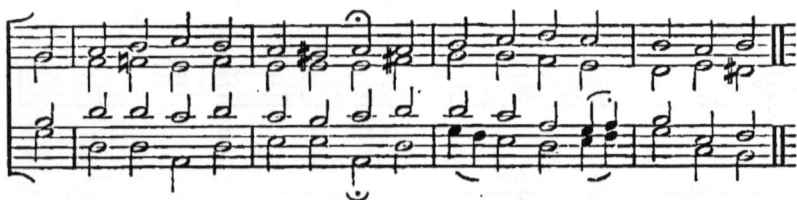

237 **Hereford.** 8.8. 8.8. 8.8.

Rev. P. La Trobe

Rochester. 8.8. 8.8. 8.8.

V. Novello.

Leader of faithful souls, and Guide
Of all who travel to the sky,
Come, and with us, e'en us abide,
Who would on Thee alone rely:
On Thee alone our spirits stay,
While held in life's uneven way.

Stella. 8.8. 8.8. 8.8.

From " Crown of Jesus " music, by permission.

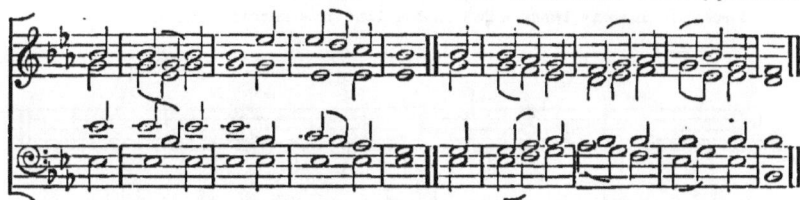

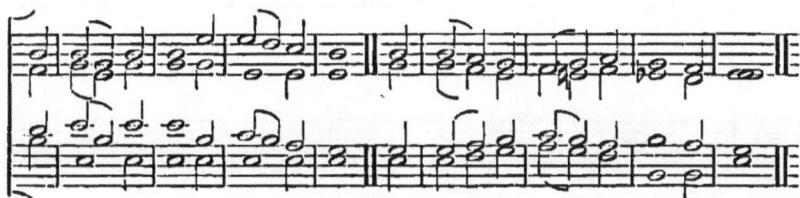

Sweet Saviour, bless us ere we go;
Thy word into our minds instil ;
And make our lukewarm hearts to glow
With lowly love and fervent will.
Through life's long day and death's dark night,
O gentle Jesus, be our light.

(163)

Braine, No. 30. 8.8.8. 8.8.8.

From W. R. BRAINE's Hymns for the Church or Home Circle, inserted by purchased permission.

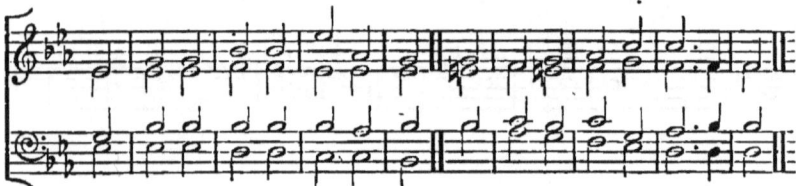

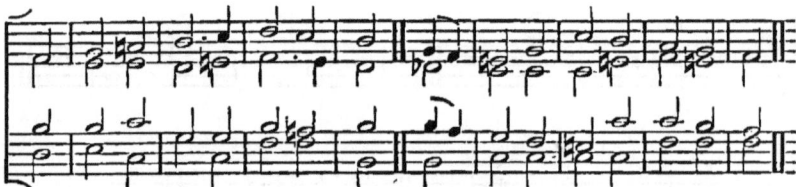

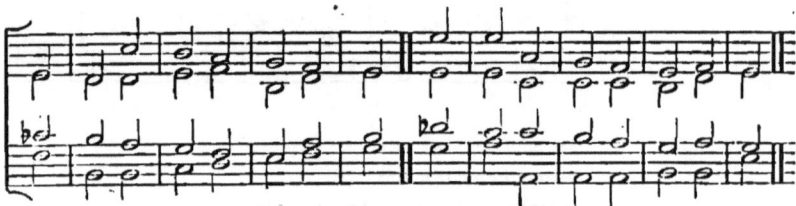

O God of gods, in whom combine
The heights and depths of love divine,
    With thankful hearts to Thee we sing;
To Thee our longing souls aspire,
In fervent flames of strong desire;
    Come, and Thy sacred unction bring.

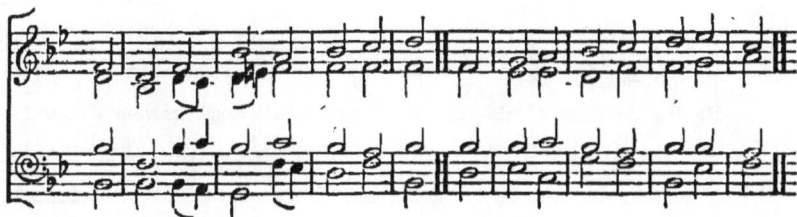

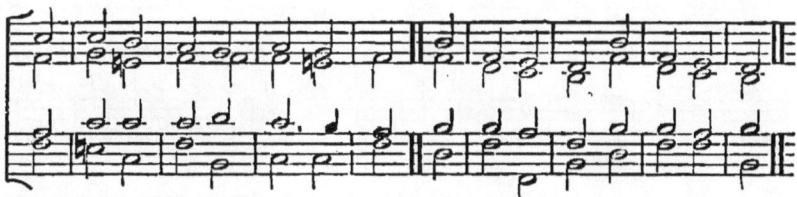

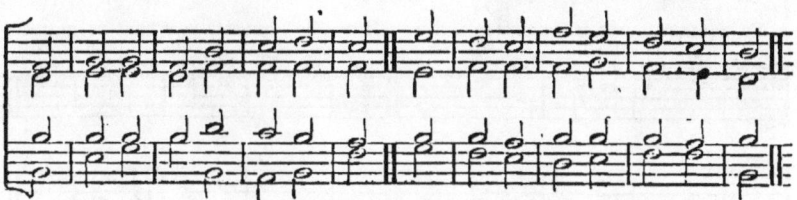

I'll praise my Maker with my breath;
And when my voice is lost in death,
   Praise shall employ my nobler powers:
My days of praise shall ne'er be past,
While life, and thought, and being last,
   Or immortality endures.

(165)

Hayes. D.L.M.

From BEETHOVEN
Arranged by W. R. Braine.

He dies, the Friend of sin-ners dies: Lo! Salem's daughters weep a - round;

A   so-lemn darkness veils the skies: A   sud-den trembling shakes the ground.

Ye saints, with con-trite hearts ro - view,   How He be-neath your burdens groaned.

Not   tears, but blood, He wept for   you,   And for a guil - ty world a - toned.

(166)

243 **Patten.** D.L.M.

W. PATTEN, Winchester.

M

244   **Cowley.**   8.8.8.8.8.8.8.8. (peculiar.)

H. B. WALMISLEY

This God is the God we a - dore, Our faithful un- change-a - ble friend;

Whose love is as great as His pow'r, And knows nei-ther mea-sure nor end.

'Tis Je-sus, the First and the Last, Whose Spi - rit shall guide us safe home;

We'll praise Him for all that is past, And trust Him for all that's to come.

Watford. 9.6. 9.6. 9.6. 9.6.

German Chorale.

O shew me not my Saviour dy - ing, As on the Cross He bled;

Nor in the tomb, a cap-tive ly - ing, For He has left the dead:

Then bid me not that form ex - tend - ed, For my Re - deem-er own;

rall.

Who, to the high-est heav'ns as - cend - ed, In glo - ry fills the throne.

246   Ellesmere.   9.8.9.8.

From MENDELSSOHN.

Bread of the world, in mercy broken,
  Wine of the soul, in mercy shed,
By whom the words of life were spoken,
  And in whose death our sins are dead ;

Look on the heart by sorrow broken,
  Look on the tears by sinners shed,
And be Thy feast to us the token,
  That by Thy grace our souls are fed.

247   Gotha.   9.8.9.8.

H.R.H. the late PRINCE CONSORT.

There is a rest from s'n and sor-row; There is a land of per-fect peace;

In patience wait, a brighter mor-row Shall bid thy toils and conflicts cease.

248 **Bremen.** 9.8.9.8.8.8.

German Chorale,
Harmony by C. H. RINK.

* ♮ according to Rink.

To Thee, O Lord, I yield my spirit,
  Who break'st in love this mortal chain;
My life I but from Thee inherit,
  And death becomes my chiefest gain.
In Thee I live, in Thee I die,
Content—for Thou art ever nigh.

(171)

249   Toulon. 10.10.10.10.

C. GOUDIMEL.

A - bide with me, fast falls the e - ven - tide; The dark-ness

thick - ens: Lord, with me a - bide: When o - ther help - ers

fail, and comforts flee, Help of the help-less, O - a - bide with me.

To these words Chant No. 262 is also suitable.

(172)

250 **Yorkshire.** 10.10.10.10.10.10.

Dr. Wainwright.

Christians, awake, salute the happy morn,
Whereon the Saviour of mankind was born;
Rise to adore the mystery of love,
Which hosts of angels chanted from above;
With them the joyful tidings first begun
Of God Incarnate and the Virgin's Son.

Streatham. 10.10.10.10.11.11.

Rev. G. T. Driffield.

On wings of faith mount up, my soul, and rise; View thine in - he-ritance be -

-yond the skies; Nor heart can think, nor mortal tongue can tell,

What end-less pleasures in those man-sions dwell. There our Re-deem-er lives, all

bright and glo-rious: O'er sin and death and hell He reigns vic - to - rious.

252

Epiphany Hymn. 11.10.11.10.

Rev. J. F. Thrupp, 1848.

Brightest and best of the sons of the morning, Dawn on our darkness and lend us Thine aid:

Star of the East, the ho - ri - zon a - dorn - ing. Guide where our in - fant Re-deem-er is laid.

253

Springfield. 11.10.11.10.

Come ye dis - con - so - late, where'er ye languish, Come, at the throne of God fer-vent-ly kneel;

Here bring your wounded hearts, here tell your anguish, Earth has no sorrow that Heav'n cannot heal.

(175)

Arley. 11.10.11.10.10.10.

A. Stone.

Draw near, ye wea-ry, bow'd and broken - heart - ed; Ye on-ward trav'llers

to a peace-ful bourne: Ye from whose path the light hath all de-part - ed:

And ye who 're left in so - li - tude to mourn: Though o'er your spi - rits

hath the storm-cloud swept, Sa - cred are sor - row's tears—since Je - sus wept.

Trinity. 11.12.12.10.

A. STONE.

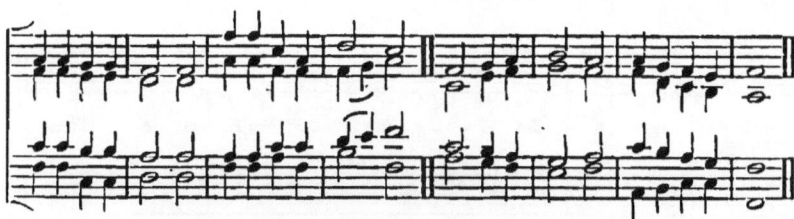

Holy, Holy, Holy! Lord God Almighty!
   Gratefully adoring our song shall rise to Thee:
Holy, Holy, Holy, merciful and mighty;
   God in Three Persons, Blessèd Trinity!

Holy, Holy, Holy! all the saints adore Thee,
   Casting down their golden crowns around the glassy sea;
Cherubim and Seraphim falling down before Thee,
   Who wast, and art, and evermore shalt be.

Holy, Holy, Holy! though the darkness hide Thee,
   Though the eye of sinful man Thy glory may not see,
Only Thou art Holy: there is none beside Thee
   Perfect in power, in love and purity.

Holy, Holy, Holy! Lord God Almighty!
   All Thy works shall praise Thy Name, in earth, and sky, and sea;
Holy, Holy, Holy! merciful and mighty;
   God in Three Persons, Blessèd Trinity!

(177)

Trinity. 11.12.12.10.

J. HOPKINS.

Published by permission of Messrs. NOVELLO & Co.

Ho - ly, Ho - ly, Ho - ly! Lord God Al - migh - ty!

Grate - ful - ly a - dor - - ing, our song shall rise to Thee.

Ho - ly, Ho - ly, Ho - ly! mer - ci - ful and migh - ty,

God in Three Per - sons, Bless - ed Tri - ni - ty!

Ems. 13.11.13.12.

German Chorale.

Thou art gone to the grave, but we will not de - plore thee,

Though sor - row and dark - ness en - com - pass the tomb;

The Sa - viour hath pass'd thro' its por - tals be - fore thee;

And the lamp of His love was thy guide thro' the gloom.

Adeste, Fideles. (Irregular.)

J. READING, 1690—1766.

O come, all ye faith-ful, joy-ful and tri-umph-ant; O come ye, O

come ye to Beth-le-hem; Come and be-hold Him, born the King of An-gels;

O come, let us a-dore Him, O come, let us a-dore Him,

O come let us a-dore Him, Christ the Lord.

(180)

Metrical Chants.

258
"Come, let us join our friends above."   S.M. or C.M.   American.

259
"Day of Wrath! that awful day,"   7.7.7.   From FELTON.

260
"My God, my Father, while I stray."   8.8.8.4. or 10.10.10.10.   W. L. REYNOLDS.

"Thy will be done."

261   8.8.8.4. or 10.10.10.10.   A. H. D. TROYTE.

262
"Abide with me."   8.8.8.4. or 10.10.10.10.   A. H. D. TROYTE.

(181)

Single Chants.

263   ALDRICH.

264   AYRTON.

265   BATTISHILL.

266   BELLAMY.

267   BLOW.

268 COOKE.

269 CROFT.

270 FARRANT.

271 FARRANT.

272 FELTON

273 W Hayes.

274 W. Hayes.

275 (Grand Chant.) P. Humphrey.

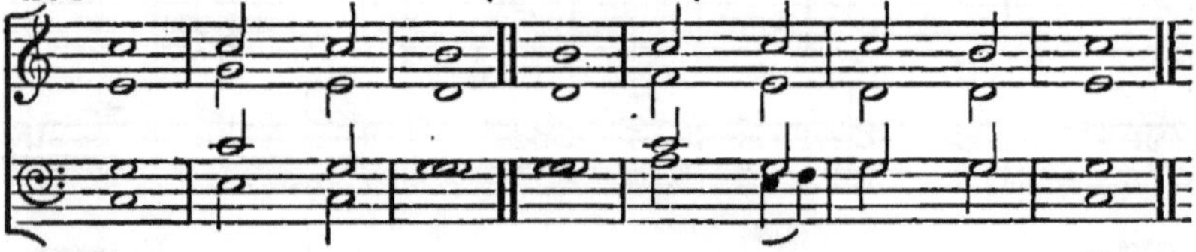

276 Kent.

277 Purcell.

278   Purcell

279   Tallis.

280   Tallis.

281   Travers.

282   Turner.

(185)

Double Chants.

283   ALCOCK.

284   BARROW.

285   BATTISHILL.

286   BATTISHILL.

287   BENNETT.

288 BLOUNT.

289 BOYCE.

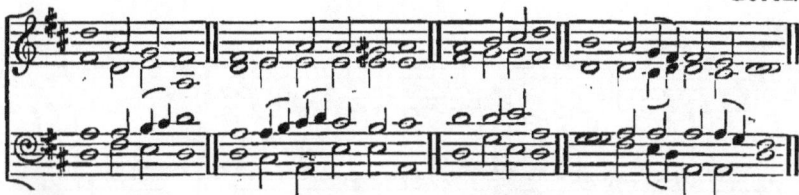

290 CALAH.

291 CALEY.

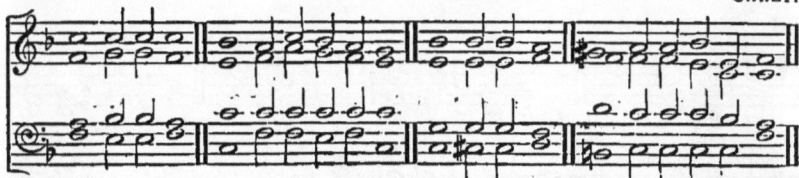

292 CALEY.
From BEETHOVEN.

293   CHARD.

294   CHARLET.

295   CLEVELAND.

296   COOKE.

297   COOKE.

298

299

CROTCH.

300

CROTCH.

301

DAVY.

302

DUPUIS.

(189)

303

GIBBONS.

304

GOODENOUGH.

305

GOSS.
From Beethoven.

306

HANDEL.

307

HEATHCOTE.

308   HENLEY.

309   JACKSON.

310   JACOBS.

311   JONES.

312   KEMP.

(191)

313

LANGDON.

314

LANGDON.

315

LAWES.

316

LESLIE.

317

LESLIE.

318

LINGARD.

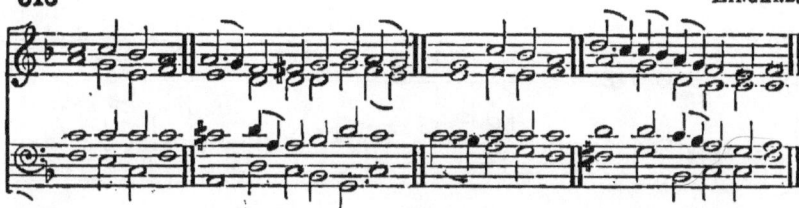

319

MORLEY.

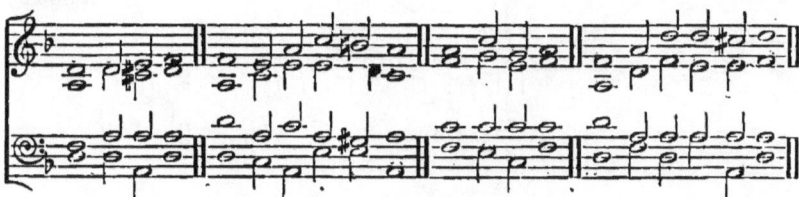

320

MORNINGTON.

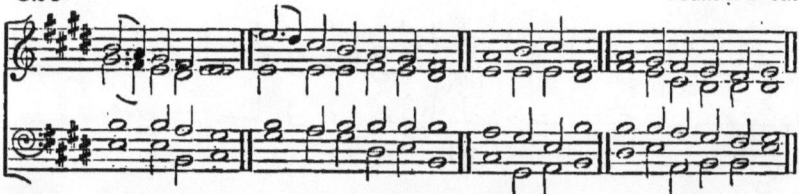

321

MORNINGTON.

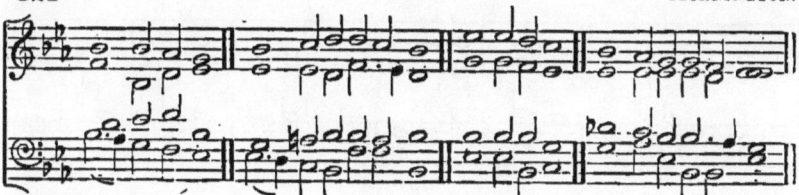

322

NORRIS

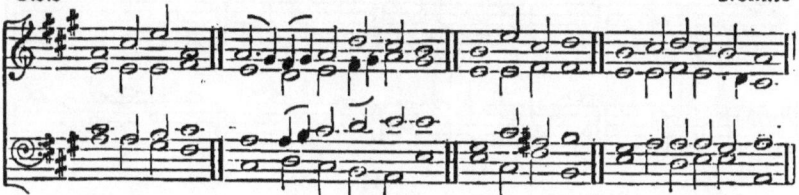

323 PEARSON.

324 RANDALL.

325 RANDALL.

326 ROBINSON.

327 ROGERS.

328   RUSSELL.

329   SMITH.

330   SPOHR.

331   WARREN.

332   WOODWARD.

(195)

Gregorian Tones. (To be sung in unison.)

333 1st Tone, 1st ending.

334 3rd Tone, 1st ending.

335 5th Tone, 1st ending.

336 5th Tone, 2nd ending.

337 6th Tone.

338   7th Tone, 1st ending.

339   7th Tone, 3rd ending.

340   8th Tone, 1st ending.

341   8th Tone, 2nd ending.

342   Tonus Peregrinus.